Eco-Chic

Elegance Renewed

by; Cole Son

#ColeSonBooks

Introduction

In the world of fast fashion and fleeting trends, the call for sustainability grows louder each day, beckoning a shift towards more responsible and environmentally friendly choices. "Elegance Renewed: Crafting Your Eco-Chic Legacy" is a manifesto and a guidebook that champions the cause of sustainable fashion, aiming to inspire readers to embrace eco-chic living with the grace of a fashion icon. This book unfolds over six meticulously curated chapters, each dedicated to exploring different dimensions of sustainable fashion and eco-conscious living. From the glamorous red carpets to the quiet elegance of everyday wear, it illustrates how sustainable practices can be woven into every thread of our lives. Through insights into the wardrobes of eco-conscious celebrities, practical green living fashion tips, and the principles of eco-chic style, this book aims to transform the way we think about fashion and our environmental footprint. It's not just about making sustainable choices; it's about becoming a sustainable fashion star in your own right, crafting a wardrobe that reflects both your style and your values. As we embark on this journey, "Elegance Renewed" serves as your compass, guiding you towards a future where fashion and sustainability are in perfect harmony.

Chapter One

The Essence of Eco-Chic

In a world where your breakfast is organic and your ride is electric, shouldn't your wardrobe reflect the same green principles? Welcome to the realm of eco-chic, where sustainability meets style with a wink and a nod, proving that saving the planet is the ultimate fashion statement.

Crafting a Personal and Sustainable Fashion Philosophy is not just about ditching plastic straws; it's a lifestyle choice that says, "Yes, I can rock this vintage jacket and save polar bears at the same time." It's about looking fabulous in pieces that have more stories than your grandmother, each thread woven with the promise of a better planet. Imagine strutting down the street in an outfit that screams, "I'm saving the world—one hemp fiber at a time!"

But how does one build this eco-friendly wardrobe without dressing like a recycled potato sack? Green Living Fashion Tips 101: Start by breaking up with fast fashion like it's that ex who never recycled. Embrace materials that love the earth back, like organic cotton, which is like the plant-based burger of textiles—good for the planet and stylish. And remember, water is for drinking, not for drowning your clothes in after one wear. Washing less is the new black.

Now, let's talk about the Must-Have Pieces for the Conscious Dresser. These are the staples of any eco-chic wardrobe, starting with the classic Little Sustainable Dress (LSD). It's versatile, it's ethical, and it pairs well with your guilt-free conscience. Next, a pair of sneakers made from recycled materials because walking the eco-talk should feel as good as it looks. And don't forget a statement tote made from repurposed billboards, perfect for carrying your eco-friendly water bottle and the weight of environmental responsibility.

Turning our gaze to the stars—not the celestial bodies, but the kind that grace red carpets and Instagram feeds—let's dive into Celebrity

Inspirations. Sustainable Celebrity Looks are not just a trend; they're a movement, led by stars who understand that being photographed in something sustainable is hotter than the latest gossip. These eco-warriors in designer clothing are showing us that you can demand attention and action for the planet, all while wearing a dress made from recycled ocean plastic.

Learning from the Red Carpet teaches us that sustainable fashion isn't just for the thrift store aficionados; it's haute couture with a heart. When your favorite celeb steps out in a gown that's both gorgeous and green, it's a powerful statement that eco-chic is ready for its close-up. It's proof that you can be part of the glitz and glamour without contributing to the landfill.

How Celebrities Are Changing the Fashion Game is a testament to their influence. They've turned the red carpet green, showing that fashion can be both aspirational and inspirational. These icons are not just wearing clothes; they're wearing their values, championing brands that prioritize the planet. It's a ripple effect that encourages designers, stylists, and fans to think differently about what they wear and why.

In conclusion, the essence of eco-chic is not just about the clothes we choose to wear; it's a statement about the world we choose to live in. It's a blend of fashion and activism that says, "Look at me, I'm fabulous and I care." So, as we navigate our way through this sustainable style journey, let's do it with a smile, because being eco-chic is not just good for the earth—it's a whole lot of fun. After all, fashion should make you feel good, inside and out, and what

feels better than saving the planet in style?

Chapter Two

Celebrity Inspirations

In the glitzy world of red carpets and paparazzi, where the flashbulbs pop faster than popcorn, a new trend is taking center stage, and it's not just another fleeting fashion fad. It's the rise of sustainable celebrity looks, where eco-friendly is the new black, and the stars are leading the charge with wardrobes that do more than just turn heads—they turn the tide on environmental degradation. Let's embark on a fabulous journey to decode how celebrities are rewriting the rules of fashion, making it cool to care and chic to conserve.

First off, "Emulating Eco-Friendly Styles of the Stars" is not about copying their homework but getting inspired by their sustainable style statements. It's like saying, "I see your eco-conscious gown, and I raise you my thrifted chic ensemble." Celebrities are donning outfits that scream (in the most sophisticated whisper), "I'm fabulous and fighting for the planet." They strut down the red carpet in dresses made from recycled plastic bottles, proving that one person's trash really can be another's treasure, especially if that other person is a fashion-forward environmentalist.

Now, let's "Learn from the Red Carpet," a veritable masterclass in sustainable fashion. This is where glamour meets green, where every step taken is a step toward a more sustainable future. It's not just about who you're wearing but what you're supporting. These events have become showcases for innovative materials, from bamboo silk to mushroom leather, teaching us that you can dazzle and be kind to the planet. Imagine a world where asking "Who are you wearing?" at the Oscars leads to a conversation about conservation and sustainability. That world is now.

The chapter on "How Celebrities Are Changing the Fashion Game" is a vibrant tapestry of tales where fashion icons and environmental advocacy weave together in a stunning eco-chic ensemble. Celebrities, with their massive platforms, are spotlighting brands that prioritize the planet, making sustainability the star of the show. They're not just walking billboards but walking billboards for change, demonstrating that style doesn't have to be sacrificed at the altar of sustainability. It's a powerful message: If they can do it under the glaring lights of fame, so can we in the audience of everyday life.

These trailblazers are doing more than just talking the talk; they're walking the walk, in ethically sourced shoes, of course. They're showing the world that being eco-conscious can also mean being fashion-conscious. It's a win-win, like finding out your favorite ice cream is also good for you. By choosing outfits that are as kind to the earth as they are eye-catching, these stars are setting a new standard, proving that true style has substance.

In the grand scheme of things, "Fashion icon eco-friendly wardrobe" is not just a trend but a movement. It's an invitation to join the ranks of those who know that fashion can be a force for good. These celebrities are not just influencers; they're inspirations, using their spotlight to illuminate the path toward a more sustainable and stylish future. They're showing that you don't have to sacrifice glamour for green, that you can have your eco-friendly cake and eat it too, in a fabulous, upcycled outfit, no less.

So, as we close this chapter on celebrity inspirations, let's take a moment to applaud these pioneers of eco-chic. They've shown us that fashion can be fun, fabulous, and fundamentally kind to the planet. It's a reminder that every choice we make, from the clothes we wear to the brands we support, is a reflection of the world we want to live in. And if the world we're striving for is one where style and sustainability go hand in hand, then thanks to these stars, we're already strutting down the right runway.

Chapter Three

Sustainable Fashion Fundamentals

Welcome to the cornerstone chapter of our eco-chic bible, where fashion isn't just about looking good; it's about feeling good and doing good too. Let's embark on a journey through the pillars of sustainable fashion, where integrating timeless pieces with trendy finds isn't just a style strategy; it's a lifestyle. We're here to redefine what it means to shop, from the thrill of the thrift to making every purchase a proclamation of our eco-conscious ethos. So, buckle up (using a recycled seatbelt, of course), and let's dive into the delightful world of sustainable fashion fundamentals.

Eco-chic style: Integrating Timeless Pieces with Trendy Finds

Imagine your wardrobe as a carefully curated art gallery, where every piece, from the timeless to the trendy, tells a story of sustainability. Integrating these finds isn't just about creating a look; it's about crafting a legacy. Think of a classic trench coat passed down through generations, paired with a chic, upcycled accessory that screams "modern muse." This isn't just fashion; it's alchemy, turning the old and the new into a gold standard for eco-chic style. It's about finding that sweet spot where your grandma's pearls meet the latest in sustainable fabric technology, proving that in the world of eco-chic, history and innovation dance together in perfect harmony.

Green living fashion tips: The Art of Thrifting and Vintage Shopping

Thrifting isn't just shopping; it's an adventure into the past, a treasure hunt where the X marks a vintage leather jacket that fits you like a glove. It's the art of finding something unique in a pile of pre-loved garments, each with a story as rich as its fabric. But this is no ordinary art; it's a sustainable one, reducing waste and giving clothes a second (or third) life. Vintage shopping is like time travel, but instead of bringing back souvenirs, you bring back fashion that stands the test of time. It's a reminder that style isn't about the price tag or the brand name; it's about the story, the sustainability, and the swagger.

Sustainable fashion like a star: Making Every Purchase Count

In the dazzling world of sustainable fashion, every purchase is a vote for the kind of world you want to live in. It's about being as discerning with your fashion choices as you are with your playlist, choosing only what you love and what loves the planet back. This isn't about mindless consumption; it's about mindful curation, selecting pieces that are not only stylish but also kind to the earth. It's a commitment to quality over quantity, to pieces that don't just fill your closet but fulfill a purpose. Making every purchase count is about wearing your values on your sleeve, literally. It's a statement that says, "I care about the planet, and my fabulous outfit is just one of the many ways I show it."

In wrapping up this chapter on sustainable fashion fundamentals, we've journeyed through the pillars that hold up the temple of eco-chic style. From integrating timeless treasures with modern masterpieces to mastering the art of thrifting, and making every purchase a pledge for the planet, we've seen how sustainable fashion is not just a trend; it's a transformation. It's a way of life that invites us to be creative, conscious, and, most importantly, compassionate. So, as we turn the page on this chapter, let's not just turn our wardrobes inside out for a fashion refresh; let's turn the fashion industry on its head with our choices. After all, in the vibrant, vivacious world of sustainable fashion, being eco-conscious is the most stylish statement we can make.

Chapter Four

Beyond the Wardrobe: Eco-Chic Living

Eco-chic living doesn't stop at your closet door. It's a lifestyle that stretches into every corner of your existence, from the products gracing your bathroom shelf to the decor that makes your home a haven. This chapter is your guide to extending that effortlessly cool, sustainable vibe beyond the wardrobe, infusing every aspect of your life with a green, glamorous glow. Let's explore how sustainable beauty rituals, eco-friendly home decor, and the green living secrets of the stars can transform not just your style, but your entire living space.

Eco-Chic Style: Sustainable Beauty and Grooming Rituals

Think of sustainable beauty and grooming rituals as the skincare routine the planet would thank you for. It's about saying goodbye to products that harm the earth and your skin, and hello to organic, cruelty-free goodies that make you glow from the inside out. Imagine slathering on a face mask made of ethically sourced honey and feeling like a queen bee or lathering up with a bar of soap that's so natural, you could almost eat it (but please, don't). This isn't just about looking good; it's about feeling good knowing your beauty routine is as clean as your conscience. Plus, who needs plastic when your beauty regime can be as zero-waste as your ambition to save the planet?

Green Living Fashion Tips: Eco-Friendly Home Decor and Lifestyle Choices

Your home is your sanctuary, so why not make it a testament to your eco-chic ethos? Eco-friendly home decor is about more than just planting a few succulents and calling it a day. It's about embracing materials that tell a story of sustainability, like reclaimed wood that adds character and history to your space, or bamboo, which grows faster than your desire to shop. It's about choosing items that not only look good but also do good, transforming your home into a showcase of sustainable living. And let's not forget the lifestyle choices that accompany this decor; from minimizing waste to embracing a plant-based diet, every choice is a step towards a more sustainable, stylish life.

Sustainable Celebrity Looks: Stars' Secrets to Green Living

Celebrities—they're just like us, but with better stylists and a slightly larger platform. When it comes to green living, they have a few tricks up their designer sleeves that can inspire us mere mortals. These stars are not just walking the green carpet; they're turning their homes and lifestyles into beacons of sustainability. From solar panels that make their homes as powered-up as their performances, to organic gardens that ensure their meals are as fresh as their film choices, celebrities show us that green living can be glamorous. They wear their eco-consciousness like a badge of honor, proving that you can live a life of luxury while still being luxuriously kind to the planet.

In the glamorous journey of eco-chic living, we learn that sustainability is not just a trend; it's a lifestyle. It's about making choices that respect the planet, from the beauty products in our bathrooms to the pillows on our couches. This chapter isn't just a guide; it's an invitation to reimagine every aspect of our lives through a green lens. By adopting sustainable beauty rituals, eco-friendly home decor, and living like the green-hearted stars, we can turn our lives into a masterpiece of eco-chic living. So, let's raise our glass (reusable, of course) to a life that's as stylish as it is sustainable, proving once and for all that when it comes to living green, the possibilities—and the fun—are endless.

Chapter Five

The Future of Fashion: Innovation and Sustainability

As we strut into the future, the fashion world is getting a green makeover, turning the runway into a greenway. This isn't just about swapping out your old threads for organic cotton tees; it's about a radical reshaping of the industry, where technological advances, sustainable brands, and visionary designers come together to stitch a new narrative for fashion. So, let's dive into the fabric of the future, where style meets sustainability, and eco-chic is the ultimate trendsetter.

Sustainable Fashion Like a Star: Technological Advances in Eco-Friendly Fabrics

Imagine wearing a dress made from algae or strutting around in sneakers crafted from air pollution. Sounds like science fiction, right? Wrong. Welcome to the future of fashion, where technological advances in eco-friendly fabrics are turning waste into want, and pollution into high fashion. These innovations are not just cool science projects; they're the building blocks of a sustainable wardrobe.

Fabrics that clean the ocean, dyes that don't poison our waterways, and materials that biodegrade with grace. This is the wardrobe of the future – where every piece tells a story of innovation, and wearing plastic bottles has never looked so chic.

Eco-Chic Style: The Rise of Sustainable Fashion Brands

Gone are the days when sustainable fashion was synonymous with hemp sacks and unflattering silhouettes. Today's sustainable fashion brands are the epitome of style, proving that you can save the planet without sacrificing your fashion sense. These brands are the rebels of the runway, challenging the status quo with every stitch and proving that green can indeed be glamorous. They're not just selling clothes; they're selling a vision of the future – one where fashion is a force for good. From luxury to streetwear, sustainable brands are popping up in every niche, catering to a growing audience of eco-conscious fashionistas who demand more from their wardrobe than just aesthetics.

Fashion Icon Eco-Friendly Wardrobe: The Role of Designers in Shaping Green Trends

Designers are the architects of the fashion world, and in the realm of sustainability, they're becoming the eco-warriors we never knew we needed. With their sketches and collections, they're painting a greener future, one where fashion doesn't cost the earth — literally. These designers are weaving sustainability into the very fabric of their creations, proving that green can indeed be the new black. They're the trendsetters, turning eco-friendly materials into covetable collections that even the most discerning fashion aficionados can't resist. Their role is pivotal because when they go green, the industry follows. And as they innovate, they inspire a whole new generation of designers to think outside the traditional textile box.

The future of fashion is bright, and not just because of the eco-friendly LED lights. It's a future where innovation and sustainability walk hand in hand down the runway, where fashion is as kind to the planet as it is to our style sensibilities. In this future, technological advances in fabrics, the rise of sustainable brands, and the visionary role of designers are not just trends; they're the new normal. So, as we look forward to this stylish, sustainable future, let's remember that fashion is not just about the clothes we wear; it's about the world we want to live in. And if this chapter is any indication, that world is going to be impeccably dressed and eco-chic to boot.

Chapter Six

Crafting Your Eco-Chic Legacy

In the grand tapestry of eco-chic living, crafting your legacy is akin to sewing the final stitch in a garment that's been lovingly crafted, piece by piece, with sustainability at its heart. This chapter isn't just about ending a narrative; it's about beginning a movement, a personal revolution that turns the act of dressing into a form of activism. So, let's dive into how engaging with the community, advocating for eco-friendly fashion, and making sustainable choices can help you leave a mark on the world, one that's as indelible as it is green.

Green Living Fashion Tips: Engaging with the Community and Spreading Awareness

Imagine if every outfit you wore could tell a story, not just of style, but of sustainability. Engaging with the community and spreading awareness about eco-chic living transforms you from a solitary eco-warrior into a leader of a green revolution. It's about hosting clothing swap parties that are so fun, they make fast fashion look like the last season. It's about organizing eco-friendly fashion shows where the runway is as green as the clothes on display. This is where your eco-chic journey becomes larger than yourself; it becomes a beacon for others to follow, showing that sustainability is not just a personal choice, but a communal celebration.

Sustainable Celebrity Looks: Becoming an Advocate for Eco-Friendly Fashion

Who says you need to be on the silver screen to influence fashion? In the age of social media, everyone's a celebrity in their own right, and you can use your platform, no matter how big or small, to advocate for eco-friendly fashion. It's about turning your Instagram feed into a parade of sustainable style, where every post is a shout-out to eco-friendly brands and practices. It's about using your voice to champion the cause, making eco-chic not just a part of your identity, but a part of your legacy. Becoming an advocate for eco-friendly fashion means you're not just wearing clothes; you're wearing your values, loud and proud, for the world to see.

Eco-Chic Style: Leaving a Lasting Impact on the World Through Sustainable Choices

The choices we make today shape the world we'll live in tomorrow. Leaving a lasting impact through sustainable choices means every purchase, every outfit, and every fashion statement is a step towards a greener, more sustainable world. It's about knowing that your eco-chic legacy is woven from the choices you make every day, from the bamboo toothbrush in your bathroom to the recycled-fiber coat in your closet. This isn't just about being remembered for your style; it's about being remembered for the difference you made, for the way you showed that fashion can be a force for good, a catalyst for change, and a testament to the power of individual action.

Crafting your eco-chic legacy is about more than just fashion; it's about forging a future where sustainability is sewn into the fabric of our lives. It's a call to action, to live and dress in ways that respect our planet and inspire others to do the same. As we close this chapter, remember that your eco-chic legacy isn't just about the clothes you leave behind; it's about the world you help to create. So, wear your eco-chic choices with pride, knowing that you're not just making a statement; you're making a difference. And in the world of fashion, that's the most stylish statement you can make.

"Elegance Renewed" not only aims to inform and inspire but also to instill a sense of responsibility and creativity in its readers. It's a guide for those who aspire to make a difference, one outfit at a time, proving that style and sustainability can coexist beautifully. Through this book, you'll discover how to embrace eco-chic living, making sustainable fashion choices that celebrate the grace of a fashion icon while caring for our planet.

Other books by Cole Son: (on amazon).

"The Santa Toy Story."

"The Owl Song."

"How I Crashed The Golden Globe Awards SIX Time."

"Think and Grow Up."

"Power OF The Thinking Mind."

"Thank You, And I Love You."

"Maliblue."

www.amazon.com/author/coleson

www.twitter.com/colesonbooks

www.instagram.com/colesonbooks

Music by Cole Son:

www.reverbnation.com/ColeSon

#ColeSon

#ColeSonBooks

Youtube: #ColeSonMusic

TikTok: @ColeSonStore

"Eco-Chic, by Cole Son.

Copyright © 2024. All rights reserved under

International and Pan-American Copyright

Conventions. By payment of the required fees, you

have been granted the non-exclusive, non-transferable

right to access and read the text of this book or e-book

on-screen. No part of this text may be reproduced,

transmitted, down-loaded, decompiled, reverse

engineered, or stored in or introduced into any

information storage and retrieval system, in any form

or by any means, whether electronic or mechanical,

now known or hereinafter invented

.